PRESENTED TO

FROM

DATE

YOUR SUPERNATURAL
RELEASE

30-Day Devotional of Prophetic Declarations

Denise Raff

Your Supernatural Release
© 2020 by GDI Enterprises, LLC

All rights reserved. No portion of this book may be reproduced, stored in a retrieval system, or transmitted in any form or by any means – electronic, mechanical, photocopy, recording, scanning, or other – except for brief quotations in critical reviews or articles, without the prior writer permission of the publisher.

Published in New Orleans, LA by GDI Enterprises, LLC.

Unless otherwise noted, scripture quotations are taken from the King James and the New Living Translation of the Holy Bible. All rights reserved.

ISBN-13: 978-0-5787-5456-7
Printed in United States of America

Hello, my name is Denise Raff, the author, I wanted to take a moment to say thank you for choosing to take a 30-day journey with me. But first...

If you are reading this book and you are not born again or saved, it is of utmost importance that you receive Jesus as Lord and Savior. God wants everyone to be saved. Today is your day of salvation. I invite you to sincerely pray and invite Jesus to come into your life to be your Lord and Savior by repeating this prayer:

Dear God,

I recognize I am a sinner in need of a Savior. I repent of my sins and ask You to forgive me. I believe Jesus died on the cross for my sins and that He was buried and that He rose again on the third day. I confess Jesus as Lord of my life and receive Him as my Savior. Help me to live for You the rest of my life. In Jesus Name, Amen.

If you sincerely prayed this prayer congratulations! You are now a child of God. Go and grow in your walk with the Lord. Find you a Bible teaching, Holy Spirit filled church by asking God to lead and show you where to go. Read your Bible and pray every day to draw closer to the Lord. Welcome to the family of God. May God abundantly bless you!

Your Supernatural RELEASE!

It is time to take a stand against the evil one and exercise the authority and dominion that was given to us by Christ Jesus because we are seated together in heavenly places in Christ. (Ephesians 2:6). The devil is defeated, and we have the victory. We must know this; believe this and act on it. Jesus paid too great of a price for us to live a defeated life.

This book is a 30-day devotional that includes scriptures, spiritual quotes as given to me by Holy Spirit and prophetic declarations to release the power of God in your life to get you through life victoriously. As you read and meditate on the words of this book daily, the power of God will be manifested in your life. Mix your faith with the Word of God and prepare for the supernatural.

God is a supernatural God who requires a supernatural people to operate in dominion and authority in the earth realm. It is His will that the people of God operate in the kingdom. Jesus prayed, "May your Kingdom come soon. May your will be done on earth, as it is in heaven." (Matthew 6:10). "For the Kingdom of God is not just a lot of talk; it is living by God's power." (I Corinthians 4:20). The Word of God also declares that the kingdom of God is righteousness, peace, and joy in the Holy Ghost. (Romans 14:17). The people of God are to be kingdom minded people; a people who are about the Father's business. We are to talk like Jesus; walk like Jesus; think like Jesus; act like Jesus and do the works that Jesus did when He walked the earth realm. In other words, Be like Jesus.

"So, God created human beings in his own image. In the image of God, he created them; male and female he created them. Then God blessed them and said, "Be fruitful and multiply. Fill the earth and govern it. Reign over the fish in the sea, the birds in the sky, and all the animals that scurry along the ground."" (Genesis 1:27-28). This was God's original intent, purpose, and plan for man. The first man Adam sinned, disobeyed, rebelled against God, and lost the dominion and authority that was given them, but the last man (Adam) Christ Jesus came and restored all that was lost. Jesus restored the kingdom and now we have the power, authority, and dominion to operate in the earth as God originally intended. So, let's do this, people of God!

Day 1

You are the light of the world—like a city on a hilltop that cannot be hidden.

No one lights a lamp and then puts it under a basket. Instead, a lamp is placed on a stand, where it gives light to everyone in the house.

In the same way, let your good deeds shine out for all to see, so that everyone will praise your heavenly Father.

Matthew 5:14-16

You are the light of the world. Light drives away darkness. If there is darkness around you, turn on the light. Shine the light that is within you, the light of the Lord Jesus Christ. Your good works will be seen, and the Father will be glorified.

PROPHETIC DECLARATIONS

In the Name of Jesus, I am the light of the world. I let my light so shine before men, that they may see my good works and glorify my Father which is in Heaven.

God is light and in Him there is no darkness. God is in me. Therefore, light is in me and there is no darkness in me. I let the light that is within me shine, shine, shine. Shine on Jesus by the power of Holy Spirit from within me. I bring light to where there is darkness.

Day 2

I press on to reach the end of the race and receive the heavenly prize for which God, through Christ Jesus, is calling us.

Philippians 3:14

Go for the gold. Whatever God called you to do, Do it! Go for it! Finish the race that is set before you with the victory. Do not leave here until your work is done. Complete your assignment. Fulfill your God-given destiny.

PROPHETIC DECLARATIONS

In the Name of Jesus, I can and will do what God called me to do. I will complete my assignment. I will fulfill my God-given destiny. Yes, I press toward the mark for the prize of the high calling of God in Christ Jesus.

Day 3

God gave Paul the power to perform unusual miracles.

When handkerchiefs or aprons that had merely touched his skin were placed on sick people, they were healed of their diseases, and evil spirits were expelled.

Acts 19:11-12

Let God do the work. The supernatural is when God intervenes and touches things. When God places His Hand on the natural, it becomes supernatural. Depend on God and not in your own ability. It is not you, but it is God working through you. It is the grace of God. Let God do it through you.

PROPHETIC DECLARATIONS

In the Name of Jesus, I am walking in the supernatural right now. God does miracles through my hands. Holy Spirit and Fire; Miracles, Signs and Wonders...this is what I want – Greater Glory!!! I allow God to do the works through me.

Day 4

Never stop praying.

I Thessalonians 5:17

Pray, pray, pray EVERY day, day, day. And when you pray, make sure you pray in faith. We must have a strong prayer life. Prayer brings God on the scene to intervene. Spend time in prayer in His presence. Cultivate your relationship with the Lord through praise and worship; get in His presence; get in His Word; get in His face. Call upon the Name of the Lord for help. Cry unto the Lord. Seek His presence daily. It is a daily walk with the Lord. Get in the secret place and stay there. The secret place is Jesus. Dwell there. Those who live in the shelter of the Most High will find rest in the shadow of the Almighty. (Psalms 91:1). Just as Jesus spent time with the Father, so should we. Be aware of the importance of prayer.

PROPHETIC DECLARATIONS

In the Name of Jesus, I pray every day. I dwell in the secret place of the Most High. The Lord abides in me and I abide in Him. I am aware of the importance of prayer. So, I spend time daily in the Lord's presence. Daily, I get in His 'Face' and in His 'Book'.

Day 5

May your Kingdom come soon. May your will be done on earth, as it is in heaven.

Matthew 6:10

God wants His Kingdom in the earth realm.
Earth should function like Heaven, and earth should look like Heaven because earth is a picture of Heaven. Whatever is going on in Heaven, it should be that way in earth. Make earth like Heaven (Heaven on earth)! The Kingdom of God is within you. Let it manifest on the outside of you. We are to advance God's Kingdom in the earth realm – manifest the kingdom in the earth now. There is no sickness, disease, fear, lack, poverty, doubt, unbelief, or anything that hurts in Heaven and it should be the same way in earth. So, our mission is to manifest the Kingdom of Heaven in earth by setting the captives free from those things that are not of God.

PROPHETIC DECLARATIONS

In the Name of Jesus, Lord, let Your Kingdom be in earth like it is in Heaven. Let Your Will be done in earth, as it is in Heaven. Thy Kingdom come, thy will be done in earth, as it is in Heaven. Let it be the way it should be like it is in Heaven. I manifest the Kingdom of God on earth right now. I go and I set the captives free. I do the works that Jesus did.

Day 6

I have told you all this so that you may have peace in me. Here on earth, you will have many trials and sorrows. But take heart because I have overcome the world.

John 16:33

You are more than a conqueror. You can overcome anything in life through Christ because He has overcome the world for us. No matter what you face in life, be of good cheer, you are a world overcomer.

PROPHETIC DECLARATIONS

If Christ has overcome the world, I have overcome the world because I am in Christ and Christ is in me. I am a world overcomer because Christ overcame the world for me. I am a world overcomer through Christ, and I win every time no matter what I face in life. Victory is mine!

Day 7

When you forgive this man, I forgive him, too. And when I forgive whatever needs to be forgiven, I do so with Christ's authority for your benefit,

So that Satan will not outsmart us. For we are familiar with his evil schemes.

II Corinthians 2:10-11

Do not be deceived. Just because something looks good, smells good and sounds good does not mean God is in it. So, be careful and do not be ignorant of the devil's devices. The devil can paint a pretty picture and make things look good when they are instead, sent to destroy you. You better recognize when it is of God and when it is of the devil.

PROPHETIC DECLARATIONS

In the Name of Jesus, I am not ignorant of the devil's devices. I recognize the things of God because I hear His voice and I know His voice and the voice of a stranger I will not follow. I am led by the Spirit of God. I follow Him. Where He leads, I will follow.

Day 8

And since we have been made right in God's sight by the blood of Christ, he will certainly save us from God's condemnation.

Romans 5:9

You are justified by the blood of Jesus. It was the blood that saved us. It was the blood that raised us. It was the blood that healed us. It was the blood that delivered us. It was the blood that set us free. It was the blood that restored us. It was the blood that redeemed us. The blood washed us and made us whole.

PROPHETIC DECLARATIONS

In the Name of Jesus, I have been justified by the blood of Jesus. I am saved, healed, delivered, restored, and set free by the blood that was shed on Calvary. The blood washed me and made me whole. I am the redeemed of the Lord for I have been redeemed from the hand of the enemy. I am in right standing with Father God.

Day 9

Daniel soon proved himself more capable than all the other administrators and high officers. Because of Daniel's great ability, the king made plans to place him over the entire empire.

Daniel 6:3

You can be excellent. The Daniel Spirit is an excellent spirit. It is a spirit of excellence. People with an excellent spirit allow God to use them. People with an excellent spirit walk in the things of God.

PROPHETIC DECLARATIONS

In the Name of Jesus, I have an excellent spirit. I walk in excellence. God uses me to do exploits and bring glory to His Name.

Day 10

Do not be afraid, for I am with you.

Do not be discouraged, for I am your God.

I will strengthen you and help you.

I will hold you up with my victorious right hand.

Isaiah 41:10

Do not be afraid. God is here. God is near and when you call on Him, He will hear. Never be afraid to be who God designed you to be and do not believe the lies of the enemy. You do not have to be afraid; you can do anything God places before you because He is with you to help you and to equip you (power and authority) to do the task at hand. You have the grace and power on the inside of you to do everything that God called you to do. He is your God; He will strengthen you; He will help you and He will uphold you with His righteous right Hand. No need to fear because God is here. He is always near. When fear comes banging on the door, send faith to answer for you.

PROPHETIC DECLARATIONS

In the Name of Jesus, I am not afraid to be who God designed me to be. I have no need to fear because God is here. He is always near. I can do anything God places before me because He is with me to help me and strengthen me. I am equipped with power and authority to do the task at hand. I have the grace to do what God has called me to do. I walk in boldness and faith, not fear.

Day 11

Fight the good fight for the true faith. Hold tightly to the eternal life to which God has called you, which you have declared so well before many witnesses.

I Timothy 6:12

Fight the good fight of faith. It is a fixed fight. We have already won because Jesus has gotten us the victory. So, walk in your victory! Do not stop fighting until you get what God has for you. He is already done it through Christ Jesus. Just receive it and accept it in Jesus' Name. Believe it and Receive it!

PROPHETIC DECLARATIONS

In the Name of Jesus, I fight the good fight of faith. I receive everything God has for me through Christ Jesus. I have the victory now because Jesus is my champion, and He has given me the victory.

Day 12

For this is how God loved the world: He gave his one and only Son, so that everyone who believes in him will not perish but have eternal life.

John 3:16

Jesus did not just die for Christians. He died for the world. He died for everyone who has ever walked the face of this earth. He loves us so much that if you were the only person who needed to be saved, He would have died for you. Now, that's Love! Jesus paid for our salvation, healing, deliverance, and victory on the cross, but it is up to us to receive it. It does not automatically happen. We got to believe it and receive it by faith. And walk in it.

PROPHETIC DECLARATIONS

In the Name of Jesus, God loved me so that He gave His only begotten Son so that I will not perish but have everlasting life. And I believe it and receive it by faith! I receive salvation, healing, deliverance, and victory now. It is mine. I take it now. I have a blood-bought, covenant right to have it.

Day 13

But when he saw the strong wind and the waves, he was terrified and began to sink. "Save me, Lord!" he shouted.

Matthew 14:30

Keep your eyes on Jesus. When Peter took his eyes off the Word (Jesus – the Living Word) and began looking at the circumstances (the Wind and the waves), he became fearful and began to sink. But as long as he kept his eyes on Jesus, he did the impossible and walked on water. The enemy tries to get you to doubt God every time. One of the greatest enemies to our faith is fear. When you are fearful, you are in doubt and unbelief and are unable to do what seems impossible. So, do not get in fear; get in faith and stay in faith. You can do the impossible if you just believe.

PROPHETIC DECLARATIONS

In the Name of Jesus, I keep my eyes on Jesus. I keep my eyes on the Word. My faith is in Jesus. My faith is in the Word and not in the circumstances. I do not go by what it looks like, but I go by what the Word says. I am not afraid because with Jesus I can do the impossible. I operate in faith, not fear. I just believe God.

_____

_____

_____

_____

_____

_____

_____

_____

_____

_____

Day 14

Love does no wrong to others, so love fulfills the requirements of God's law.

Romans 13:10

Love is the fulfilling of the law. Jesus came to fulfill the law. Love, Jesus, fulfilled the law. If you truly love with the Love of God, you will not break the law or the commandments of God. To love Him is to obey Him. Jesus said in John 14:15, "If you love me, obey my commandments."

PROPHETIC DECLARATIONS

In the Name of Jesus, I love with the Love of God and I obey His commandments because Love is the fulfilling of the law. I love the Lord and I obey the Lord. I walk in Love just as Christ loves me. Lord, I thank You. I hear from You and I do what You say do.

Day 15

And "do not sin by letting anger control you." Do not let the sun go down while you are still angry, for anger gives a foothold to the devil.

Ephesians 4:26-27

Tell the devil to shut up! Be gone and leave me alone. When the devil reminds you of your past, remind him of his future – he has no future just like you have no past. The devil is defeated. So, do not let him win by believing his lies.

PROPHETIC DECLARATIONS

In the Name of Jesus, I give no place to the devil. I do not give in to the temptations of the devil. I command you devil to shut up; be gone and leave me alone. In Christ, I have no past just like you have no future. Now go away in Jesus' Name.

Day 16

For every child of God defeats this evil world, and we achieve this victory through our faith.

I John 5:4

Better days are ahead. If you are a born again, child of God, you have overcome the world. You have the victory through your faith. Whatever you are going through, you are coming out with the victory. Know that it is going to be better than it was before. Whatever it is, it will not be like this always. Your breakthrough is on the way.

PROPHETIC DECLARATIONS

In the Name of Jesus, I am an overcomer because I am a born again, child of God. I have overcome the world through faith in Christ. I have the victory that overcomes the world. I am walking in victory now. My breakthrough is on the way.

Day 17

Do everything without complaining and arguing, so that no one can criticize you.

Philippians 2:14-15

Hush. Stop murmuring and complaining and get to worshiping and praising. Train yourself to go from worry to worship, from a negative attitude to praise. Be grateful and thankful for what you do have. Do not worry about what you do not have. Get your focus right. Keep your focus on Jesus.

PROPHETIC DECLARATIONS

In the Name of Jesus, I do not murmur and complain. I worship and praise the Lord. I am grateful and thankful for what I have. My focus is on Jesus. I keep my eyes fixed on the Lord and not on the problems that I am facing.

Day 18

Today I have given you the choice between life and death, between blessings and curses. Now I call on heaven and earth to witness the choice you make. Oh, that you would choose life, so that you and your descendants might live!

Deuteronomy 30:19

Choose life says the Lord. Anything in life can be used for good or evil. It is a choice. Speak life over circumstances. Be careful of the words that you speak. You can create your world with the words you speak. Make sure they are God's Words – words that line up with the Word of God because God's Words are life. God's Words are good. So, you can have a good life by speaking God's good Words.

PROPHETIC DECLARATIONS

I choose life not death. I choose blessing not cursing that both I and my children may live. I speak life over circumstances. I create the world that I desire with my words – words that line up with the Word of God. God's Words and blessings are manifesting in my life now.

Day 19

So, if the Son sets you free, you are truly free.

John 8:36

We are free. Jesus set us free when He died on Calvary. We are free from sickness and disease. We are free from fear. We are free from lack. We are free from everything that is not of God. No longer in bondage but free, free, free.

PROPHETIC DECLARATIONS

In the Name of Jesus, I am free! Free! Free! Jesus set me free. I am free from sin. I am free from sickness and disease. I am free from fear. I am free from anything that is not of God. Now I can set others free by the blood of Jesus and the power of Holy Spirit.

Day 20

The tongue can bring death or life; those who love to talk will reap the consequences.

Proverbs 18:21

You must speak life. Words have creative ability, power, and authority. You create with the words you speak whether negative or positive. So, watch what you say. Be careful of the words that you speak. You want the life of God not death operating in your life.

PROPHETIC DECLARATIONS

I create with the words of my mouth. I speak life. I speak the best. I speak positive words. I speak the Word of God over situations and circumstances I face in life. The life of God is operating in me.

Day 21

For God has not given us a spirit of fear and timidity,

but of power, love, and self-discipline.

II Timothy 1:7

Do not be afraid. Fear is an enemy that does not come from God. Jesus defeated fear at the cross. So, you do not have to fear. Just ignore fear and act like it does not exist because it does not. It does not exist in God, the kingdom nor Heaven. Therefore, it does not exist in you because God is in you; the kingdom is in you and Heaven is in you. When fear knocks, send faith to answer the door and tell it where to go – back to the pit from where it came and shut the door on fear.

PROPHETIC DECLARATIONS

In the Name of Jesus, I will not fear; for God has not given me the spirit of fear; but of power, and of love and of a sound mind. I have victory over fear because Jesus defeated fear at the cross. I resist fear. I ignore fear and act like fear does not exist because it does not. It does not exist in God. God is in me. Therefore, fear does not exist in me.

Day 22

So, let us come boldly to the throne of our gracious God. There we will receive his mercy, and we will find grace to help us when we need it most.

Hebrews 4:16

Boldness is your God-given right. We can come boldly to the throne as if we have done nothing wrong. Jesus made a way for us to come into the Father's presence at any time. Whenever you need grace; whenever you need mercy, come to the throne of grace, and receive it.

PROPHETIC DECLARATIONS

In the Name of Jesus, I come boldly to the throne of grace, that I may obtain mercy, and find grace to help in time of need. I come to the throne as if I have done nothing wrong because the blood of Jesus cleanses me from all unrighteousness and washes away all my sins. I go to the Father in a time of need.

Day 23

Once you were dead because of your disobedience and your many sins.

Ephesians 2:1

Jesus delivered us from sin. When we were dead in sin, He made us alive again. We are dead to sin and alive unto God. Therefore, sin cannot have dominion over us.

PROPHETIC DECLARATIONS

In the Name of Jesus, I was dead in sin, but God made me alive again. I am dead to sin. I am alive in Christ Jesus. Sin cannot have dominion over me. I am free from sin.

Day 24

But Christ has rescued us from the curse pronounced by the law. When he was hung on the cross, he took upon himself the curse for our wrongdoing. For it is written in the Scriptures, "Cursed is everyone who is hung on a tree."

Through Christ Jesus, God has blessed the Gentiles with the same blessing he promised to Abraham, so that we who are believers might receive the promised Holy Spirit through faith.

Galatians 3:13-14

We are redeemed! Christ redeemed us and set us free when He hung on that tree. We are redeemed from the curse of the law. We have been redeemed from the hand of the enemy. We are free from any and everything that is not of God. Let the redeemed of the Lord say so.

PROPHETIC DECLARATIONS

In the Name of Jesus, Christ has redeemed me from the curse of the law. I am redeemed from sin. I am redeemed from sickness and disease. I am redeemed from poverty and lack. I am redeemed from spiritual death (separation from God). I have been redeemed from the hand of the enemy and I have the promise of the Spirit through faith.

Day 25

God is not a man, so he does not lie.

He is not human, so he does not change his mind.

Has he ever spoken and failed to act?

Has he ever promised and not carried it through?

Numbers 23:19

God cannot lie. It is impossible. If He said it, He will do it. If He spoke it, He will bring it to pass. He will make it good in your life. Whatever God says, you can bank on it. Just trust Him! He is faithful! He is reliable! He is trustworthy! He will never let you down or disappoint you!

PROPHETIC DECLARATIONS

In the Name of Jesus, I trust in the Lord because it is impossible for Him to lie. My faith is in the Lord. My hope is in the Lord. I can depend on the Lord. He is faithful and will not let me down. He will never disappoint me.

Day 26

Do not worry about anything; instead, pray about everything. Tell God what you need and thank him for all he has done.

Then you will experience God's peace, which exceeds anything we can understand. His peace will guard your hearts and minds as you live in Christ Jesus.

Philippians 4:6-7

He is the God of peace. There is a peace that only God can give. God's peace surpasses all understanding. You can have peace even in the midst of turmoil. Do not worry about anything. Pray about everything and the peace of God will keep and guard your heart and mind through Christ Jesus.

PROPHETIC DECLARATIONS

In the Name of Jesus, I have the peace of God. God's peace surpasses all understanding. I do not worry about anything, but I pray about everything and the peace of God keeps and guards my heart and mind through Christ Jesus.

Day 27

But Jesus told him, "No! The Scriptures say,

'People do not live by bread alone, but by every word that comes from the mouth of God.

Matthew 4:4

His Word is life. Get in the Word and live by the Word of God. It is life for God is the life-giving source.

PROPHETIC DECLARATIONS

In the Name of Jesus, I live by the Word of God. God's Words are spirit, and they are life for He is the life-giving source.

Day 28

For as he thinketh in his heart, so is he: Eat and drink, saith he to thee; but his heart is not with thee.

Proverbs 23:7 KJV

Think. You will eventually become what you think. So, think on good things, God things. Think on things that are true; things that are honest; things that are just; things that are pure; things that are lovely; things that are of a good report (Philippians 4:8); for as you think in your heart, so are you. Fill your heart with the Word of God so that you can think on the Word of God.

PROPHETIC DECLARATIONS

In the Name of Jesus, I think in line with the Word of God. I fill my heart with the Word of God so that I can think on the Word of God. I think on things that are good, true, honest, just, pure, lovely and of a good report. And I am starting to look like who God says I am.

Day 29

My child, pay attention to what I say.

Listen carefully to my words.

Do not lose sight of them.

Let them penetrate deep into your heart, for they bring life to those who find them, and healing to their whole body.

Proverbs 4:20-22

His Word heals. God's Word is medicine to all our flesh. Take your medicine (scriptures) daily and walk in divine health.

PROPHETIC DECLARATIONS

In the Name of Jesus, God's Word is my medicine. I take my medicine daily by reading, studying, and meditating on the Word of God and I walk in divine health. Healing is the children's bread. I have a blood bought covenant right to be healed. I am healed by Jesus' stripes and I have the life of God.

Day 30

At the very moment they began to sing and give praise, the Lord caused the armies of Ammon, Moab, and Mount Seir to start fighting among themselves.

II Chronicles 20:22

Praise wins battles. Praise confuses the enemy. Praise causes your enemies to turn against each other and destroy one another. Praise is evidence that you have faith. Let God know you trust Him by praising Him! Oh, He loves it when we praise Him! If you praise Him, He will come see about you and see you through with the victory!

PROPHETIC DECLARATIONS

In the Name of Jesus, God, I praise You because I trust You. You are awesome. You are great. You are mighty. There is none like You. None can be compared to You. You are bigger than anything. You are greater than anything. You are the Great I AM. I praise you for the victory and I bless Your Holy Name! (Now is a good time to continue to praise Him with your own words of praise and adoration – spend about 30 seconds praising Him for His goodness.)

Conclusion

These prophetic declarations can also be used as prayers in your prayer time. Meditation of the Word of God is so important. The Bible teaches that we have what we say. When we begin to speak the Word of God, the Word of God begins to manifest in our lives. God's Word works. We just got to work it. Act on the Word. Obeying the Word of God gives us complete victory. I pray this devotional blesses you as you speak the Word of God over your life and the lives of your loved ones. Keep trusting; keep believing; keeping speaking the Word of God and watch things change in your life for the better and line up with the Word of God as you release the supernatural in you.

About the Author

Denise Raff is a wife, mother, licensed minister, intercessor, and prophetic believer. She is an alumnus of Wossman High School and holds a Bachelor of Science Degree from Grambling State University. Her hobbies include reading, singing, traveling, and spending time with her family. She loves the Lord and loves ministering to people. Her mission in life is to impart healing, deliverance, and restoration to the lost, hurting and dying.

Denise Raff may be reached at the following:

Facebook: Wonderful Life in Christ Ministries with L. Denise Raff

YouTube Channel: Wonderful Life in Christ Ministries – L. Denise Raff

Instagram: @wonderfulifeinchristministries

Email: wonderfulifeinchrist@gmail.com

www.ingramcontent.com/pod-product-compliance
Lightning Source LLC
Chambersburg PA
CBHW071405290426
44108CB00014B/1689